THE COMPLETE GUIDE TO
HORSES

Sandy Creek
NEW YORK

An Imprint of Sterling Publishing Co., Inc.
1166 Avenue of the Americas
New York, NY 10036

SANDY CREEK and the distinctive Sandy Creek logo are
registered trademarks of Barnes & Noble, Inc.

Text © 2016 by QEB Publishing, Inc.
Illustrations © 2016 by QEB Publishing, Inc.
Photography © 2016 by Bob Langrish, Shutterstock and Getty Images

Design & Editorial: Cloud King Creative
Picture Research: Susannah Jayes and Cloud King Creative

This 2016 edition published by Sandy Creek.

ISBN 978-1-4351-6355-3

Manufactured in China
Lot #:
4 6 8 10 9 7 5 3
05/17

THE COMPLETE GUIDE TO
HORSES

NICOLA JANE SWINNEY
AND BRENDA APSLEY

Sandy Creek
NEW YORK

CONTENTS

Words in **bold** are explained in the Glossary on page 138.

BY OUR SIDE

Without the horse, the world we live in today would be very different. Since humans first realized that these animals would make an ideal form of transportation, equines have been our constant companions. They have been by our side in war, in adventure, in sports, and in leisure throughout our history.

Shaped by Places and People

The climate and terrain have shaped the breeds of each country, from the Arabian of the desert, which has contributed so much to the world's equines, to England's hardy little Exmoor pony.

But we have shaped the horse for our own needs, too. The **heavy horses** needed to carry armored warriors into battle have been replaced by the sleek **Thoroughbred** for racing, and the athletic warmblood for **competition**. The beauty of the black Friesian adds pomp to ceremonial carriages, and the Lipizzaner dances for our entertainment.

An elegant competition breed in action.

In Praise of the Horse

We are lucky that such creatures, whose size and strength could easily overcome us, are happy to work with us and for us. Ronald Duncan said it best in his poem *In Praise of the Horse* in 1954: "Where in this wide world can man find nobility without pride, friendship without envy, or beauty without vanity? Here, where grace is laced with muscle and strength by gentleness confined..."

A fine cavalry horse on duty.

Shire horses working the land.

7

HORSES AND PONIES

Horses and ponies belong to the same family, **Equidae**. They are the same sort of shape and live in the same sort of way. The main difference is size—horses are larger than ponies.

Horses are measured using a measuring stick.

8

Horse or Pony?

Size is the not the only distinction between the two—also look at breed and fit. Imagine an adult on an equine's back—if it seems a good fit, it's probably a horse. Another clue is **withers**—14.2hh is 4' 10", so if the equine's withers come to the shoulders of someone 5' 2" tall, it's probably a pony.

A heavy draft horse.

A white horse meets a white Shetland Pony.

A horse is usually 14.2hh or taller and a pony shorter than that, at maturity. In some parts of the U.S. ponies are 14.1hh.

Little and Large

Horses and ponies are measured in **hands**—a hand being 4 inches, expressed as h (hand/s) or hh (hands high) followed by a point, and the number of added inches. A horse measuring 15.2hh is 15 hands tall, plus 2 inches, a total of 62 inches. Measurement is from the ground to the withers (the highest part of the back at the base of the neck).

POINTS OF A HORSE

A horse's **conformation** is its shape and form, for example shape of neck and length of back. A specialized vocabulary is used to name specific parts—the **points**—of a horse or pony.

Left and Right

The left side of a horse is the near side and the right is the off side. Riders usually lead and get on a horse from the near side.

Bones

The bones that make up a horse's skeleton are what give it shape, support its body, and protect organs like the heart, and liver.

loins

croup

dock

tail

flank

stifle

gaskin

hock

fetlock

pastern

hoof

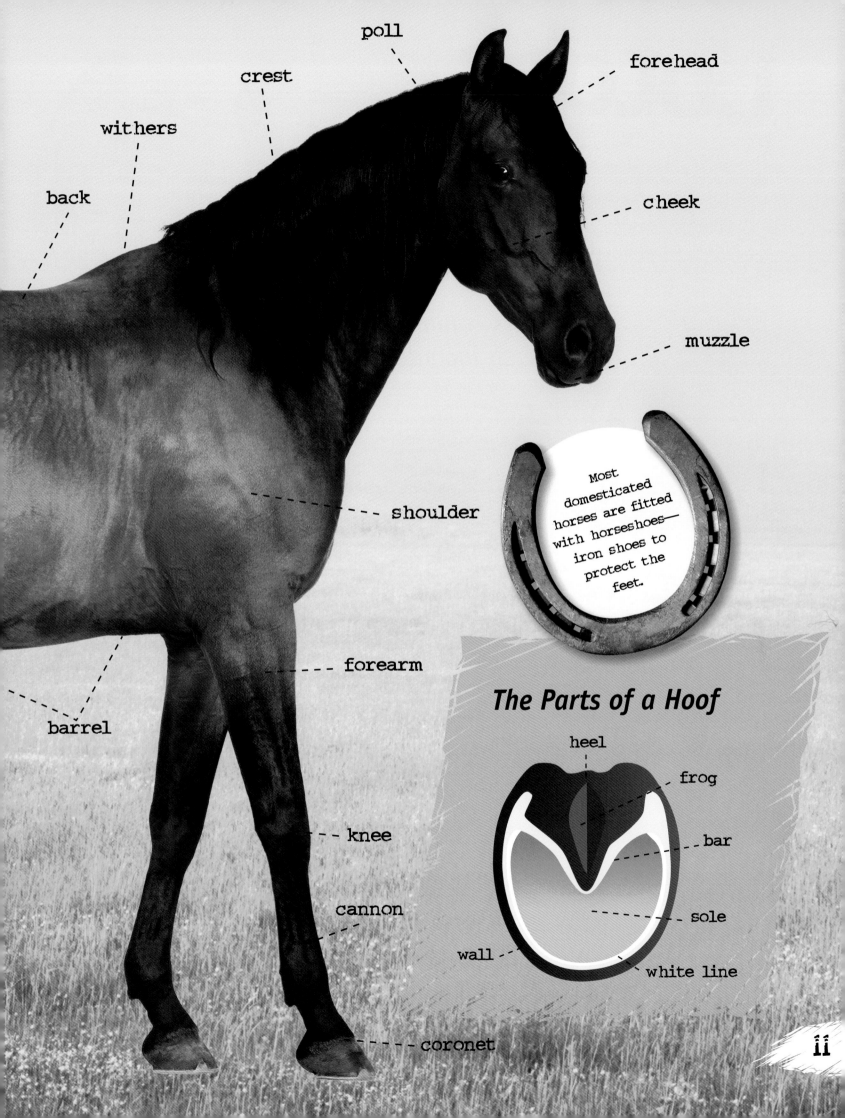

poll

crest

forehead

withers

back

cheek

muzzle

shoulder

Most domesticated horses are fitted with horseshoes— iron shoes to protect the feet.

forearm

barrel

The Parts of a Hoof

heel

frog

knee

bar

cannon

sole

wall

white line

coronet

COLORS

Horses can be classified by coat color, breed, and sex. Color is a key descriptor—some breeds must be certain colors, while in other breeds a range of colors is allowed.

Colors commonly seen include:

Chestnut
Reddish with no black, mane and tail same shade or lighter than body coat.

Bay
Light red-brown to very dark brown, with black points (mane, tail, lower legs). Variations include dark and blood.

Roan
White hairs evenly mixed with body color hairs, head usually solid color or darker than body. Variations include red, bay, and blue. True whites, with white hair and pink skin, and blue or brown eyes, are rare. Most white horses are gray with a full coat of white hair.

Gray
Black skin with white hair, or a mix of dark and white hairs. Can be born any color, lightening with age. Variations include salt and pepper, dapple, and rose.

Black

True blacks must be completely black, but can have markings. Variations include fading and non-fading.

Dun

Yellowish coat, darker mane and tail, stripe along the backbone darker than body coat.

Pinto

Broad spotting patterns, with brown, white and/or black and white patches. Variations include **piebald** and **skewbald**.

Brindle

Faint vertical stripes slightly lighter than base coat.

Palomino

Golden or tan with cream or white mane and tail.

Appaloosa

Dark leopard-style spots all over body, on lighter base coat.

MARKINGS

White markings are unique to every horse. Together with eye color (especially blue), **whorls** and **chestnuts**, present at birth and throughout life, make up a horse's identity or **passport**.

White facial markings, described by shape and location, include:

Strip or Stripe
Narrow stripe down middle of face.

Bald
Wide area starting above forehead, extending to side of face.

Blaze
Wide area down middle of face, along nose.

Star
Marking or spot on forehead above or between eyes.

Snip
Marking or spot on muzzle between or below nostrils.

White leg markings, described by highest part of leg covered, include:

Stocking
Edge of hoof to knee or hock.

Sock
Edge of hoof to **fetlock**—can also be a boot.

Pastern
Extends above top of hoof, but stops below fetlock.

Coronet
Narrow band, marking or ring just above hoof.

Whorls and Chestnuts

Other unique marks are whorls—also called crowns, swirls, or cowlicks—patches of hair growing in the opposite direction to the rest, often on the face, stifle, or hock. Chestnuts are rough patches on the inner leg, sometimes compared to fingerprints in humans.

This horse has a whorl on his head.

White markings are usually white hairs on pink skin.

15

HORSE BREEDS

Horses and ponies come in different shapes and sizes. Some belong to a distinct breed, where they share the same characteristics as other horses or ponies of that breed. Characteristics include horse colors, **temperament**, and **gait**. Horses are divided into three groups—**hotblood**, **coldblood**, and **warmblood**. Pony breeds are not categorized this way.

A graceful, galloping chestnut hotblood.

Hotbloods

Hotbloods originate from the Middle East and North Africa. A lack of good grazing and a harsh climate produced a fast, lean, and hardy horse. Hotbloods commonly possess beauty and elegance.

Coldbloods

Coldblood horses typically come from northern Europe, where the cool, rainy climate yields rich grazing. These horses are often large and stocky, and possess great strength.

Warmbloods

Warmblood breeds were produced by crossing hotbloods and coldbloods. They are usually middle-weight horses and are bred for sport, primarily **showjumping** and **dressage**.

A fine German warmblood competes at an show-jumping event.

The Palomino is a famous warmblood breed.

Ponies

Ponies are of course smaller than horses, but height is not the only factor that differentiates these two animals. Ponies have thicker manes, coats, and bones, making them appear plumper and stockier than horses. Ponies have a more gentle disposition and are less volatile, making them much more manageable than horses. But despite these differences, ponies and horses share a similar lifespan—both will live until around 25 to 30 years of age.

Two ponies gently grooming each other.

COMPETITION BREEDS

Special competition and sport breeds feature in equestrian events including dressage (performing complex movements), showjumping (jumping fences) and **eventing** (showjumping, dressage, and cross-country).

Look for the rosettes throughout the book, to see the competition events for which a horse is bred.

KNOWN FOR:
- Dressage
- Showjumping
- Driving

The highest price paid for a thoroughbred race horse at public auction is $16 million for a two-year-old, unnamed colt, who had yet to race.

Breeding

Competition breeds are bred for conformation and movement (affecting jumping ability, etc.), but also temperament, as intense training requires willing, obedient horses.

Trakehner

The Trakehner, from East Prussia, has been successful in dressage, **driving**, showjumping, and eventing competitions to Olympic standard.

Hanoverian

The Hanoverian is an ultra-versatile competition horse, combining power, athletic **action**, and a good nature.

Holstein

Germany's Holstein or Holsteiner is highly adaptable, the perfect partner for the skilled showjumper or cross-country rider.

Dutch Warmblood

The Dutch Warmblood was bred in the Netherlands, from Groningen, Gelderlander, and Thoroughbred blood. It is a bold, brave showjumper with a calm temperament.

FOUNDING BREEDS

Most modern breeds of horses are based on the Arabian. This includes the mighty Thoroughbred, which in turn has influenced other breeds and is still used to refine more common stock.

ARCTIC
OCEAN

EURASIA

Andalusian
SPAIN

EUROPE

Akhal-Teke
TURKMENISTAN

AFRICA

INDIAN
OCEAN

Thoroughbred
SYRIA

Arabian
SAUDI ARABIA

21

ARABIAN

SAUDI ARABIA

The Arabian is believed to be the oldest breed of horse in the world today. It was bred to be a desert horse and can live on little food. Because it lived close to the Bedouin—traveling desert people—it developed a bond with humans. It dates back more than 5,000 years and has influenced many modern breeds.

Bedouin breeders prized the Arabian above rubies. They decorated their horses with colorful tack—rosettes, beads, shells, and tassels.

Elegant Mover
The Arabian horse's action is so smooth that it is said to float. It also has another desirable trait called "elevation", meaning its trot is high off the ground. The breed has great speed and stamina, too.

The Arabian's head is easily recognizable. It has large, beautiful "liquid" eyes, small, neat ears, and wide nostrils.

The shield-shaped "jibbah" on its forehead is unique to Arabians. It is a feature that breeders and owners value.

KNOWN FOR:
- Dressage
- Showjumping
- Driving

Clever Horse

Fast learners, Arabian horses are easy to train, but fiery and highly strung, too. They bond with their owner or trainer and are loyal and affectionate. Often unpredictable, Arabians are not always suitable for beginner riders, but they do make great competition horses.

AKHAL-TEKE

TURKMENISTAN

Some people believe this glorious breed is even older than the Arabian. The bones of these tall, finely boned horses were found in southern Turkmenistan in central Asia, dating from 2,400 B.C. With its clean, spare lines and shimmering coat, it rivals the Arabian for beauty and grace.

The Legend

This breed has always hit the headlines. When Melekush was given as a gift to Queen Elizabeth II in 1956, her grooms thought that the horse's beautiful gleaming coat had been polished. They gave it a bath—which made its coat shine all the more.

The Name

The word "Akhal" comes from a long oasis in the foothills of the Persian Kopet Dag Mountains. "Teke" is after the nomadic Turkmen people who lived and bred their unique horses there. Turkmenistan is isolated, with the Caspian Sea to the west, mountains to the south, and desert to the north. The breed has remained largely free of outside influence.

The Akhal-Teke is said to be an intensely loyal, 'one-man' horse.

KNOWN FOR:
- Dressage
- Showjumping
- Racing

The Fame

The Akhal-Teke was prized by rulers throughout history. Alexander the Great's magnificent horse Bucephalus is thought to have been an Akhal-Teke. The breed was also used by Genghis Khan, Marco Polo, Roman emperors, and many more. Some historians say the Byerley Turk, one of the founders of the Thoroughbred breed, was actually an Akhal-Teke.

THOROUGHBRED

SYRIA

Horse racing is one of the biggest equine "industries" in the world. People gamble huge sums of money on the outcome of contests between these beautiful creatures. Many of these ultimate athletes are Thoroughbreds—the product of four centuries of selective breeding.

Original Arabian blood gave the Thoroughbred speed, stamina, and undeniable beauty.

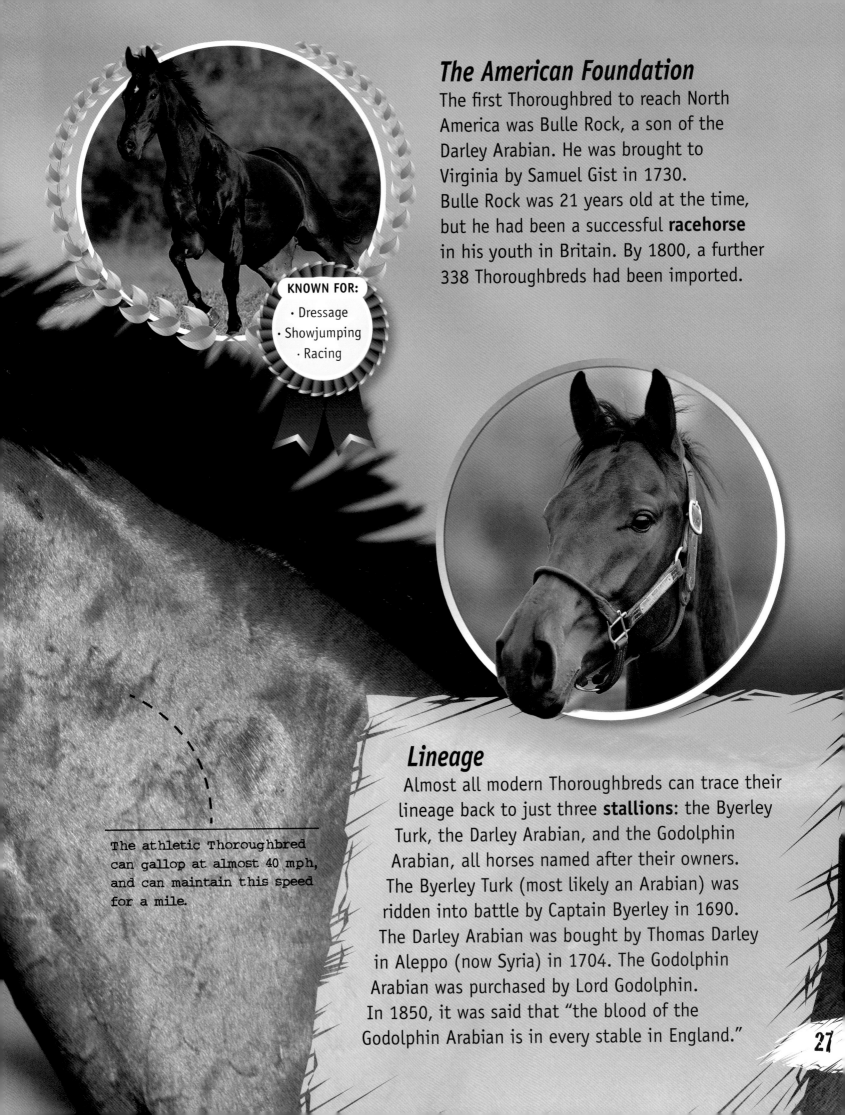

The American Foundation

The first Thoroughbred to reach North America was Bulle Rock, a son of the Darley Arabian. He was brought to Virginia by Samuel Gist in 1730. Bulle Rock was 21 years old at the time, but he had been a successful **racehorse** in his youth in Britain. By 1800, a further 338 Thoroughbreds had been imported.

KNOWN FOR:
- Dressage
- Showjumping
- Racing

The athletic Thoroughbred can gallop at almost 40 mph, and can maintain this speed for a mile.

Lineage

Almost all modern Thoroughbreds can trace their lineage back to just three **stallions**: the Byerley Turk, the Darley Arabian, and the Godolphin Arabian, all horses named after their owners. The Byerley Turk (most likely an Arabian) was ridden into battle by Captain Byerley in 1690. The Darley Arabian was bought by Thomas Darley in Aleppo (now Syria) in 1704. The Godolphin Arabian was purchased by Lord Godolphin. In 1850, it was said that "the blood of the Godolphin Arabian is in every stable in England."

27

ANDALUSIAN

SPAIN

The Andalusian is a magnificent athlete: a perfect, living machine and the very picture of equine beauty. The seamless bond early warriors had with this breed of horse is thought to be where the myth of the centaur—half man, half horse—came from.

The Andalusian is a superb athlete. It has long, sloping shoulders with prominent withers, rounded hindquarters, and strong legs with short cannon bones.

This attractive horse is known as the aristocrat of the equine world.

History

Horses lived on the Iberian Peninsula—Spain and Portugal—as far back as 25,000 B.C. The Andalusian was prized as a cavalry horse and was the chosen horse of European rulers. But the breed nearly died out because of cross-breeding, and being used so much in the Napoleonic wars. Luckily, a group of monks saved the Andalusian, and ensured the bloodlines were not lost.

KNOWN FOR:

- Dressage
- Showjumping
- Driving

Set on an arched and powerful neck, the head is balanced and refined without being dainty.

Dressage Dream

The Andalusian's dazzling, high-stepping action can really cover ground. The horse is at its best in the fiestas—or festivals—in its Spanish homeland, but it also excels in the show ring and the dressage arena.

29

WILD AND FERAL HORSES

Sadly, there are no longer any truly "wild" equines. Humans have been so successful in domesticating the horse that even those that roam free are **feral**: the descendants of once tame horses and ponies that have returned to their natural, wild state.

Mustang
U.S.A.

Exmoor
ENGLAND, U.K.

NORTH
AMERICA

ATLANTIC
OCEAN

EUROPE

New Forest
ENGLAND, U.K.

AFRICA

Chincoteague
U.S.A.

Brumby
AUSTRALIA

Camargue
FRANCE

31

MUSTANG

U.S.A.

The Mustang is the unofficial national horse of the United States, having roamed free across the country for centuries. Originally brought to the Americas in the 1500s by Spanish explorers, the name "Mustang" comes from the Spanish word *mesteño*, meaning "wild" or "stray".

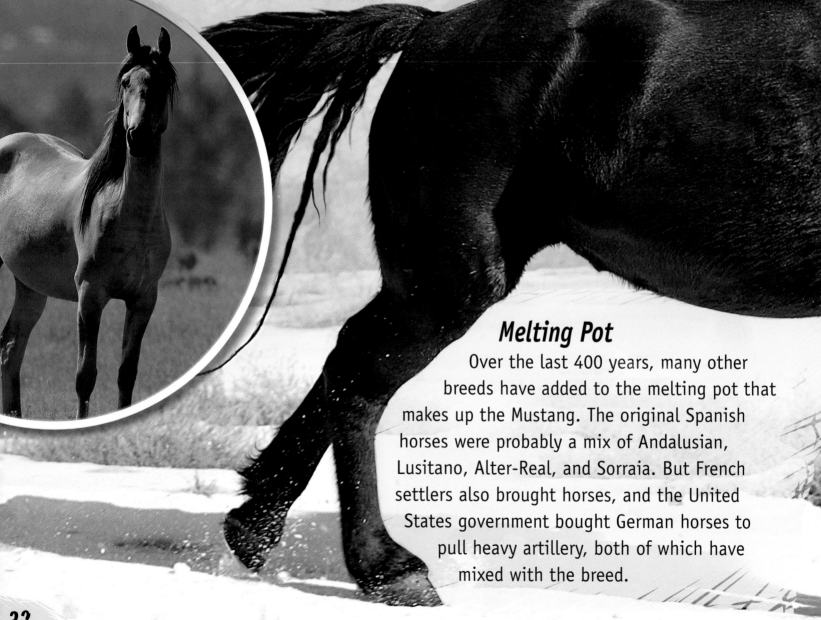

Melting Pot
Over the last 400 years, many other breeds have added to the melting pot that makes up the Mustang. The original Spanish horses were probably a mix of Andalusian, Lusitano, Alter-Real, and Sorraia. But French settlers also brought horses, and the United States government bought German horses to pull heavy artillery, both of which have mixed with the breed.

A Mustang's head is usually dainty, like a pony.

Threat

Mustangs were previously thought of as pests. In the early 1900s, when food was scarce, cattle had to share the plains with around two million wild horses. Ranchers shot the horses, creating more grazing for their cattle. Today, the Mustang is protected by law.

Many colors appear in the modern Mustang, including piebald and skewbald. The occasional gray-dun or grullo can still be seen—echoing the original Sorraia horse.

CHINCOTEAGUE

Marguerite Henry's novel *Misty of Chincoteague* ensured that this little creature, who actually lives on Assateague Island, off the coast of Virginia, has a lasting place in our hearts. But no one really knows how the ponies came to be on the island in the first place.

Child's Pony
Although the Chincoteague is actually a feral horse, it is gentle and calm, making an ideal child's pony. Standing around 12 to 13 hands tall, it is suited to smaller riders. It can survive on little, and is less expensive to keep than some breeds.

Island Life

The island of Assateague is shared between the states of Maryland and Virginia. One herd lives at the Maryland end, while another lives at the Virginia end. Each summer, the Virginia herd is swum across a channel to the nearby Chincoteague Island by "saltwater cowboys," before thousands of spectators.

Legend tells that the ponies came to the island from a wrecked Spanish galleon. *La Galga* sank off the coast of Virginia in 1750.

The Future

Once the ponies reach Chincoteague, the **foals** are auctioned off. Around 70 foals are born every year and three-quarters of them will be sold. Some will be "buybacks"—the new owner agrees to give the pony back to the herd to keep the bloodlines healthy.

35

BRUMBY

AUSTRALIA

There are various stories that explain how the iconic wild horse of Australia got its name. There were no horses on this vast continent until the "First Fleet" of ships from Great Britain landed in 1788. These ships contained convicts who had been deported, along with livestock and supplies. The early horses were of Thoroughbred blood and only the toughest survived the long, hard voyage.

The name "Brumby" may also have originated from "baroomby," the Aboriginal word for "wild."

The Myth Behind the Name

Their new world was huge and largely barren. Many horses soon escaped and became feral. British soldier and farrier, James Brumby, owned several horses. He moved from New South Wales to Tasmania in the 19th century, leaving some horses behind. When people asked who the horses belonged to, they were told "they're Brumby's."

Mobs or Bands

Brumby horses became plentiful in Australia. They were fast, hardy, and resourceful, evading capture. Because they were inbred, they kept their wild tendencies and proved difficult to tame, making them unsuitable as riding horses. They traveled in large groups—known as mobs or bands—each of which had a senior stallion, **mares**, young **colts**, and **fillies**. In time, these colts would fight the stallion for control of the band.

Harsh Realities

Unfortunately, the wild Brumby was considered a pest, and still is by many. They compete with livestock for meager food supplies and precious water. Their hard hooves wear paths through the outback, and they can spread disease. Numbers are controlled by the Australian government. There are thought to be at least 600,000 wild Brumbies in Australia today.

CAMARGUE

FRANCE

These ghostly "Horses of the Sea" move through the mist at the delta of the Rhone River in southern France. These are the Camargue horses, named after marshland where the Rhone meets the Mediterranean. The breed is one of the oldest in the world. Equines have existed in this unforgiving region since prehistoric times, and the Camargue is thought to have descended from the now-extinct Solutré Horse, about which little is known.

Ancient History

Throughout history, many armies have passed through this region, including the Greeks, Romans, and Arabs. The horses they brought with them undoubtedly had some influence on the Camargue, although there is little evidence of Arabian blood. But they have remained remarkably uniform. It has also been suggested that the Camargue has influenced the horses of Spain, since the invading armies took some animals home when they returned.

White Horses

Camargue horses run wild in small herds across the marshes, which are either scorched by the sun or lashed with icy winds blowing off the Alps. The herds are formed of a stallion, his mares, and their offspring. Foals are born from April to July, and are dark brown or black. Their coat lightens with age, until they become almost pure white in maturity. Shaped by their harsh environment, they are small, but tough and hardy.

In 1928, the wetlands where the Camargue horses roam were declared a national park, and the horses became a protected species.

EXMOOR

ENGLAND, U.K.

Some 100,000 years ago, horses arrived in what is now England. They crossed the swampy land that later became the English Channel, long before the country was cut off from the rest of Europe. Those first equines are thought to have changed very little. Evidence dating back over 60,000 years reveals horses that bear a strong resemblance to the Exmoor pony of today.

Isolated Isles

The world changed a great deal through the millennia, with various invading armies and foreign equine blood influencing British breeds. But on inhospitable Exmoor, in the West Country of England, the wild ponies were largely free from outside influence. No new breeds were introduced to refine or improve existing stock.

The Exmoor is considered "critical" by the Rare Breeds Survival Trust. During World War II, the wild ponies were used as target practice. By the end of the war, only around 50 remained.

The ponies today still live free on the moor, but they are carefully monitored by the Exmoor Pony Society.

Built to Last

Few creatures are better designed to survive harsh conditions than the Exmoor pony. Its eyes are hooded to protect them from snow and wind. It grows a thick, double-layered coat in the winter to keep it warm and dry, and its tail has a snow-chute (also called an ice-tail)—a group of short, coarse hairs at the top, designed to draw snow and ice away from its body. This, and the double-layered coat, are shed in the summer, to be regrown in the autumn.

NEW FOREST

ENGLAND, U.K.

Ponies have roamed the forests of southern England since the end of the last Ice Age, roughly 10,000 years ago. These are known as the New Forest ponies, or simply "Foresters," and without them the New Forest itself would be very different—more overgrown, with fewer birds and flowers. The ponies' and the forest's fortunes are intertwined.

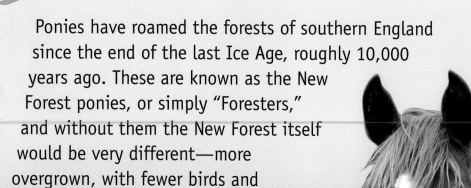

Ancient History

Bones of a pony standing around 13hh were found at a Roman villa in Rockbourne, Hampshire. Centuries later, the profits of the Royal Stud at nearby Lyndhurst went toward building Beaulieu Abbey, founded in 1204. The earliest record of ponies in the New Forest is from 1016, when the rights of common pasture allowed local people to graze their animals in the forest.

In 1765, an attempt was made to improve the breed's bloodline by introducing a famous Thoroughbred called Marske.

Uncertain Future

There are thought to be fewer than 3,000 breeding adult ponies, making the New Forest's future look uncertain. They still roam free there, but are owned privately by the local Commoners. Each fall, the ponies are checked over for general health and treated if necessary.

AMERICA'S HORSES

There were no horses at all in the Americas until the late 15th century, but the range of breeds now found there is truly impressive. American breeders have produced some of the most glorious equines in the world.

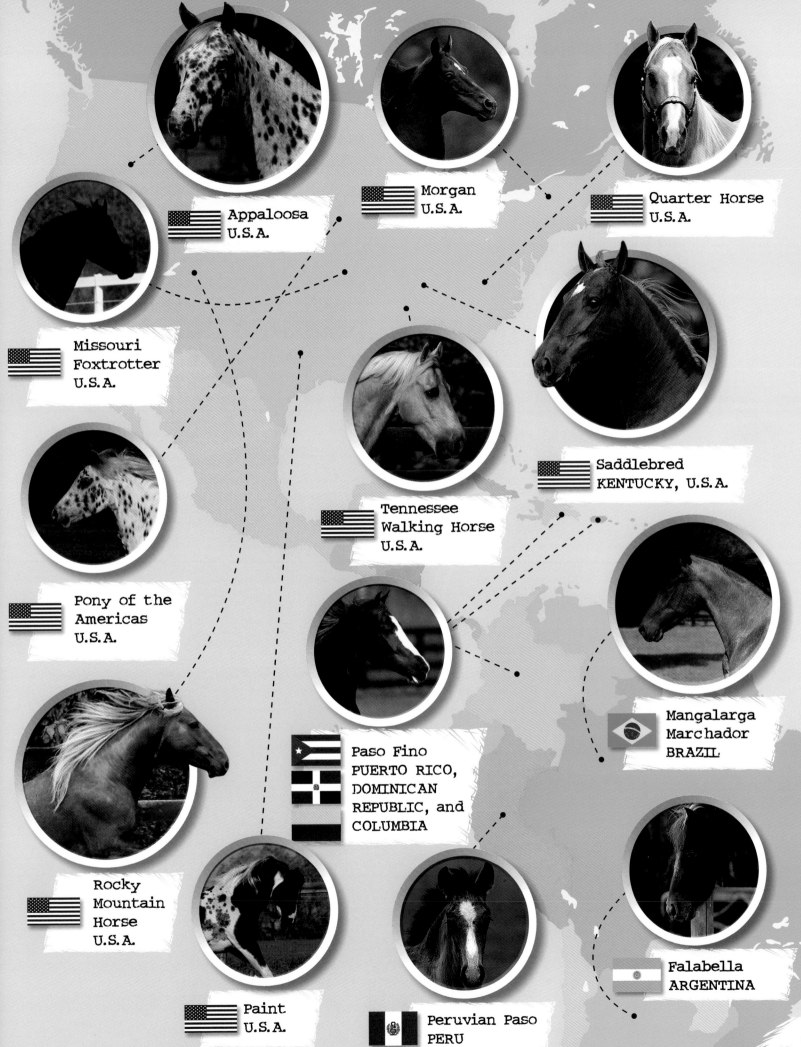

Appaloosa
U.S.A.

Morgan
U.S.A.

Quarter Horse
U.S.A.

Missouri
Foxtrotter
U.S.A.

Saddlebred
KENTUCKY, U.S.A.

Tennessee
Walking Horse
U.S.A.

Pony of the
Americas
U.S.A.

Mangalarga
Marchador
BRAZIL

Paso Fino
PUERTO RICO,
DOMINICAN
REPUBLIC, and
COLUMBIA

Rocky
Mountain
Horse
U.S.A.

Paint
U.S.A.

Peruvian Paso
PERU

Falabella
ARGENTINA

MORGAN

VERMONT, U.S.A.

In the past, animals were often named after their owners. The legendary horse that was the start of a famous American breed was known as "the Justin Morgan horse," even though his real name was Figure. And "legend" is not too strong a word: this powerful, compact little creature was renowned far and wide.

KNOWN FOR:
- Dressage
- Showjumping
- Driving

The Beginning
Figure belonged to Justin Morgan of Vermont and is thought to have been foaled in 1789. His sire was a stallion called True Briton, also known as Beautiful Bay. True Briton was an English Thoroughbred. The resulting colt was to go on to found America's first horse breed.

The Legend

Stories of "the Morgan horse's" strength, speed, and stamina quickly spread. His owner raced him and hired him out for farm work. At barely 14hh, he seemed tireless and could out-walk, out-trot, out-run, and out-pull almost every other horse. His offspring resembled him, both in looks and nature.

Figure himself lived to the age of 32, despite a lifetime of hard work.

The Breed

Figure's foals were in demand and the "Morgan horses" became recognized as a breed. They were compact and hardy, but refined and elegant in appearance. Their sweet temper and trainability were much admired.

47

QUARTER HORSE

VIRGINIA, U.S.A.

One of the most iconic American breeds, the Quarter Horse gets its name from the distance of one-on-one races that were popular in the late 1600s. Horses were run along tracks of a quarter-mile. The fastest animals were known originally as Celebrated American Running Horses.

Big Business

Huge bets were placed on these races—some of the grand plantations may have changed hands as a result of these contests! Disagreements were common, although the quality of the horses was one thing everyone agreed on. As well as being fast, these compact horses were good-looking, too.

The Modern Breed

With its combination of speed and strength, the Quarter Horse is admired worldwide. The breed has a calm temperament, making it ideal for the beginning rider. Its versatility makes it suitable for work or pleasure.

KNOWN FOR:
- Dressage
- Showjumping
- Driving

It is said that the Quarter Horse is able to "stop on a dime" from a full gallop.

Moving West

During the 1800s, huge cattle ranches were set up all over the Western Plains. The Quarter Horse, which had great stamina, also proved to have another desirable trait—"cow sense," or the ability to out-maneuver cattle. Agile and easy to train, it soon became popular with ranchers.

49

TENNESSEE WALKING HORSE

TENNESSEE, U.S.A.

Few American breeds are more instantly recognizable than the Tennessee Walking Horse, sometimes known as "the Walker." It was the first horse breed named after a U.S. state. It is one of the many **"gaited"** horses—those that possess another gait or gaits as well as the standard walk, trot, canter, and gallop.

Beginnings

Various breeds came together to make the modern Tennessee Walker. Among them were the now-defunct Narragansett Pacer, Canadian Pacer, Morgan, Standardbred, and Saddlebred. The Walking Horse was popular with plantation owners, who needed a comfortable mode of transportation to carry them around their land.

The beautiful modern Walker has an elegant head, intelligent eye, and long graceful neck.

The Gaits
The Tennessee Walking Horse has three exceptional gaits— the flat-foot walk, the running walk, and a smooth canter. It is most famous for the running walk. Smooth and gliding, the horse can reach speeds of up to 20 mph. All gaits are inherited, not taught.

SADDLEBRED

KENTUCKY, U.S.A.

This breed, which has its roots in the 1600s, was originally known simply as "the American Horse." It is based on the gaited horses known as Narragansett Pacers, founded in Rhode Island, and crossed with Thoroughbreds. The new breed became more refined than the Pacers, but retained their comfortable gait. High-stepping and elegant, the Saddlebred is the ultimate show horse.

KNOWN FOR:
- Dressage
- Showjumping
- Riding

The Versatile Breed
Whether in the dressage arena, eventing, showjumping, endurance riding, or driving, the Saddlebred excels.

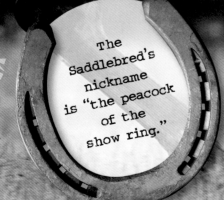

The Saddlebred's nickname is "the peacock of the show ring."

52

The Comfortable Pace

Like all of America's gaited breeds, the Saddlebred moves its legs at the same time on each side. This is different from the lateral trot, in which the front and hind legs move on the diagonal. This reduces jolting, and makes for a supremely comfortable gait.

History on His Back

These "American Horses" carried the Colonial cavalry to victory over the British in the Battle of King's Mountain in South Carolina in 1780. And in the Civil War, American generals rode Saddlebreds, among them General Robert E. Lee's famous Traveler. After the war, the soldiers took their horses home with them, to spread the breed across the United States.

MISSOURI FOXTROTTER

MISSOURI, U.S.A.

The Missouri Foxtrotter, the official state horse since 2002, was bred by settlers in the Ozark Mountains in the early 19th century as a fast, reliable stock horse, distinguished by its "foxtrot" gait.

KNOWN FOR:

• Endurance riding

The "foxtrot"

The "foxtrot" gait differs from the trot in other breeds, described as the horse walking with its front feet and trotting with its hind feet, one front foot on the ground at all times. The gait produces little bounce in the horse's back, and thus a smooth ride.

Stock Horse

Mid-sized and muscular, the Foxtrotter is the perfect ranch horse, pulling plows, hauling logs, but above all working with cattle. Good-looking, with a neat head, pointed ears, and tapered muzzle, it is graceful and relaxed in motion, with a gentle disposition—ideal for disabled and young riders. The U.S. Forest Service used this reliable breed to make the first horseback descent of the north rim of the Grand Canyon in Arizona.

The Foxtrotter can maintain speeds of 5–8 mph and can cover short distances at up to 10 mph.

ROCKY MOUNTAIN HORSE

ROCKY MOUNTAINS, U.S.A.

The Rocky Mountain Horse (R.M.H.) of the Appalachian Mountains in the U.S. state of Kentucky is valued for its versatility, kind nature—and attractive good looks.

KNOWN FOR:
- Trail
- Endurance racing

All-arounder

Averaging 14.2–16hh, these horses were perfect for farms in the local "rocky mountain" terrain of their breed name. Hardy enough to survive winter weather with little shelter and able to plow, work cattle, and pull carts, today they excel in trail, and endurance riding.

"Chocolate"
All solid colors of R.M.H. are allowed, but especially prized is the dark brown "chocolate" color (silver dapple on black base coat) with pale flaxen mane and tail. Some white markings are permitted, but not leg markings above the knee.

The R.M.H.'s natural four-beat ambling gait (the "single foot") requires minimum effort from horse and rider, enabling them to cover great distances without tiring.

Old Tobe
Most of today's Rocky Mountain Horses can be traced back to a stallion called Old Tobe. Used by breeder Sam Tuttle as a sure-footed, intelligent, and gentle trail horse, these qualities passed to his descendants.

57

APPALOOSA

IDAHO, U.S.A.

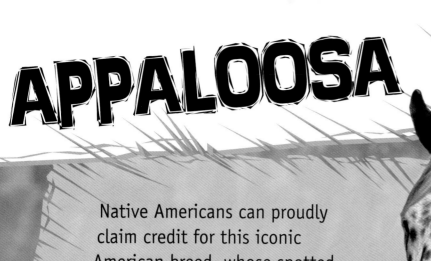

Native Americans can proudly claim credit for this iconic American breed, whose spotted coat is prized around the world. The Nez Percé were the only tribe to selectively breed their horses. They wanted the best—the strongest, fastest, and most sure-footed.

Distinctive Patterns

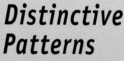

Instantly identifiable by its spots, the Appaloosa must have three other characteristics: white **sclera** (around the eye), mottled skin, and striped hooves. The main markings are: **blanket**, spots, blanket with spots, roan, roan blanket, roan blanket with spots, and solid.

KNOWN FOR:
- Dressage
- Showjumping
- Racing

The breed gets its name from the Palouse River. Settlers referred to "a Palouse horse," which later became "apalousey horse," and finally, Appaloosa.

Colorful History

The Nez Percé entered into a treaty with the U.S. government in 1855, which gave the tribe millions of acres of land. But in 1860, gold was discovered on the reservation, which brought an influx of settlers, breaching the treaty. The tribe's lands were reduced, and battles broke out. The chief surrendered in 1877 and the tribe's horses were confiscated. The Nez Percé were banned from owning the breed, a law that stood until 1991.

FALABELLA

Small but mighty, the Falabella is most definitely a horse, not a pony, despite its tiny frame. Like most American breeds, it originated from the Spanish horses brought to the New World in the 16th century, some of which were either released or escaped.

Tough Existence

They were undoubtedly shaped by their harsh environment. The Argentinian pampas plains offered little food or water, so the herds had to travel huge distances. Those that faltered did not make it. Those that were left—short in stature, stocky, and tough—formed the modern Falabella. Inbreeding among the herds may also have restricted their size.

Tiny Horses

In the 1840s, an Irish settler in Argentina, Patrick Newell, began a breeding program with the small horses found around Buenos Aires. An expert horseman, he passed his knowledge, and herd, to his son-in-law, Juan Falabella. This began a family tradition of breeding and exporting the tiny horses.

Other equine blood was used over the centuries, including the tough Criollo (Argentina's national breed), Appaloosa, and Welsh Mountain pony.

PONY OF THE AMERICAS

IOWA, U.S.A.

A foal called Black Hand founded America's favorite pony breed. A Shetland breeder from Iowa named Les Boomhower was offered an Arabian/Appaloosa mare who had been bred to a Shetland stallion. When the foal, a colt, was born, its coat was white with black splashes, one of which looked like a handprint. Les named it Black Hand.

KNOWN FOR:
- Dressage
- Showjumping
- Racing

How it Began

Boomhower contacted other Shetland breeders and they formed the Pony of the Americas Club in 1954. His vision was to produce a pony breed for children to ride and show—adults could only show the ponies in-hand or driven. To be suitable for children, the pony had to be gentle and easy to train.

Strict Guidelines

For an animal to be registered as a Pony of the Americas (P.O.A.), it has to be between 44 and 52 inches in height. Its head should be small and dished—or concave—like that of an Arabian, and its body muscled like a Quarter Horse. It must also have Appaloosa-like markings, visible from 40 feet.

The modern P.O.A's maximum height is 56 inches. Less Shetland blood is used, with more Welsh, Quarter Horse, and Appaloosa, to achieve the look of a little horse rather than a pony.

PASO FINO

PUERTO RICO

DOMINICAN REPUBLIC

COLOMBIA

Known as the "horse of the fine walk," the Paso Fino is one of the most celebrated gaited breeds of the Americas. On his second voyage to the Americas in 1493, Christopher Columbus brought a group of horses from Spain, and settled them at Santo Domingo, Dominican Republic. They were a mix of Spanish breeds, including the now-extinct Jennet.

In addition to its fine gait, the beautiful Paso Fino is athletic, with great stamina, yet is kind and gentle. It can adapt to different climates and uses, and can now be found throughout North and South America.

Handsome and Refined

The Jennet was rather plain, but it had a particularly comfortable and smooth four-beat gait that it passed on to its offspring. Mixing with other breeds produced a handsome, refined creature that had a *paso fino*, or "fine step." When the foals are born and struggle to their feet, they move naturally in this gait.

Best-kept Secret

Perhaps the Americas' best-kept secret, the Paso Fino is quickly gaining a reputation as the "smoothest riding horse in the world." Its supremely comfortable gait is a lateral pace, with little up-and-down movement in the hindquarters or in the horse's shoulders, making for a smooth ride. Its "fine step" is unique to the breed.

KNOWN FOR:
- Dressage
- Endurance riding

65

PERUVIAN PASO

PERU

Although it shares some common ancestry with the Paso Fino, Peru's national horse is an entirely separate breed. The first horses to arrive in Peru came with Francisco Pizarro in 1531. On these unfamiliar mounts, Pizarro's troops terrified their Inca enemies, who had never seen such creatures.

Just forty or so years ago, the Peruvian Paso was virtually unheard of outside Peru. It remained pure for four centuries, and its wonderful, smooth gait is guaranteed to be passed on to its offspring.

After the Incas

After the fall of the Inca Empire, the conquistadors' horses were still vital for communication, but the Spanish soon found another use for their mounts—on their vast plantations, which were then more common than ranches. The long distances they needed to cover resulted in the development of the modern Peruvian Paso.

KNOWN FOR:
- Dressage
- Showjumping
- Driving

Small and Smooth

Long distances needed a horse with stamina, and long hours spent in the saddle required a comfortable ride. The difficult terrain, with its narrow mountain passes and dense rain forest, required a smaller horse than the taller breeds used on ranches. An athletic, lighter creature with a smooth pace was much better suited to life in Peru.

MANGALARGA MARCHADOR

BRAZIL

Just saying the name of Brazil's national horse makes you want to dance! And that's what these beautiful horses seem to do: the word *marcha* describes their smooth and rhythmic gait. "Mangalarga" comes from the farm where many of the early horses were bred. Carefully kept records means that modern Marchadors can be traced back twenty generations or more.

In 1994, two Brazilian men completed an 8,694-mile trail ride to prove the breed's stamina. For 18 months, they rode all day and rested all night, using the same horses.

Royal Beginnings

When Napoleon's armies threatened Portugal in 1807, the royal family fled to Brazil, taking their best horses with them. These included a stallion called Sublime, who was crossed with Brazil's existing horses, which were mostly of Spanish stock. The resulting animals were initially known as "Sublime horses".

The Marcha Gaits

There are three *marchas*: the *marcha picada*, which is described as a broken pace, with more lateral movement than diagonal; the *marcha batida*, which is the opposite; and the *marcha de centro*, where the lateral and diagonal movements are equal. In all *marcha* gaits, the horse always has some contact with the ground, so the rider feels secure.

KNOWN FOR:
· Endurance riding
· Showjumping
· Dressage

PAINT

U.S.A.

Herds of colored horses once roamed the plains and deserts of North America, but were later domesticated. Native Americans believed the striking, broken-coated horses to have magical powers. The Comanche tribe, considered to be the finest riders of the American plains, possessed many of these creatures. The horses are depicted on the painted buffalo robes the tribe used as historical records.

Herding and Ranching

Of Spanish origin, introduced to the New World by the conquistadors, this tough little horse was prized by the cowboys for its strength and agility. Many of the colored horses that roamed so freely in the 1800s were of "stock" type—compact, strong, with good bones and a sound constitution. They made excellent cow ponies, for herding and ranching cattle.

KNOWN FOR:
· Dressage
· Showjumping
· Rodeo

The Modern Paint

The first official American Paint Horse was a black-and-white tobiano stallion called Bandits Pinto, owned by the Flying M Ranch of McKinney, Texas. It was recorded in 1962, when a society to protect the breed was started. The association wanted to ensure that the breed was not solely based on coat patterns, so set strict standards of conformation, athletic ability, temperament, and performance.

The terms "piebald" and "skewbald" originate from the word "bald" used to describe a white face.

The Patterns

There are two main types of coat pattern in the modern Paint horse—tobiano and overo. The tobiano horse has a solid-colored head, sometimes with a star or blaze, four white legs, strong markings, including dark flanks, and its tail is often two colors. The overo has no white on its back between the withers and the tail, one or all four legs is dark, its markings are splashy, and its face may be white.

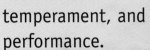

HORSES FROM AROUND THE WORLD

Icelandic
ICELAND

Connemara
IRELAND

Clydesdale
SCOTLAND, U.K.

Highland
SCOTLAND, U.K.

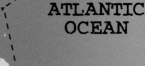
ATLANTIC
OCEAN

Shetland
SCOTLAND, U.K.

Arabian influence stretches across the globe, from the mighty Percheron of France, to the pretty Welsh Mountain pony of the United Kingdom, and the handsome, fleet-footed Orlov Trotter of old Russia. The beauty of the world's horses is glorious in its diversity.

72

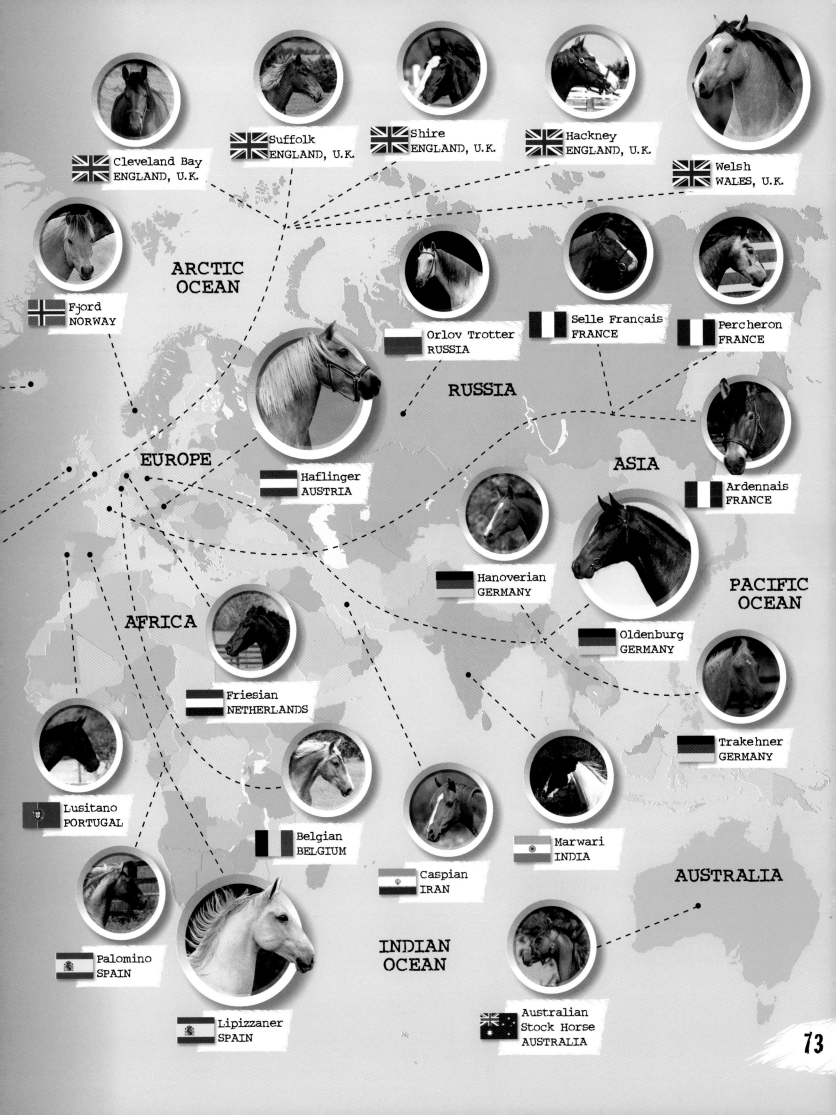

Cleveland Bay
ENGLAND, U.K.

Suffolk
ENGLAND, U.K.

Shire
ENGLAND, U.K.

Hackney
ENGLAND, U.K.

Welsh
WALES, U.K.

Fjord
NORWAY

ARCTIC
OCEAN

Orlov Trotter
RUSSIA

Selle Français
FRANCE

Percheron
FRANCE

RUSSIA

EUROPE

Haflinger
AUSTRIA

ASIA

Ardennais
FRANCE

AFRICA

Hanoverian
GERMANY

PACIFIC
OCEAN

Oldenburg
GERMANY

Friesian
NETHERLANDS

Trakehner
GERMANY

Lusitano
PORTUGAL

Belgian
BELGIUM

Caspian
IRAN

Marwari
INDIA

AUSTRALIA

Palomino
SPAIN

INDIAN
OCEAN

Lipizzaner
SPAIN

Australian
Stock Horse
AUSTRALIA

73

LIPIZZANER

SPAIN

The Lipizaner breed was founded by Archduke Charles II, brother of the Roman Emporer Maximilian I, at the court stud farm of Lipizza, Italy, in 1580. The stud farm still exists today, in what is now Lipica, in Slovenia. The farm's "dancing white horses" were showcased in the Spanish Riding School, performing "high school," movements and "airs above the ground."

KNOWN FOR:
- Dressage
- Showjumping
- Racing

Spanish and Arabian

The Lipizzaner has great strength and nobility, thanks to its Spanish heritage and Arabian blood. White horses have always been prized—they pulled royal chariots and have represented peace and justice since Roman times.

74

Mixed Origins

Just six stallions founded the modern Lipizzaner—known best for their performances as part of the Spanish Riding School of Vienna. The stallions were Conversano, a black horse of Arabian origin; Favory, a dun; Maestoso, a white horse of Spanish descent; Neapolitano, a bay; Pluto, with Danish blood; and the Arabian gray, Siglavy.

Though the Lipizzaner is found in Europe, the U.S. and Canada, it is relatively rare, with only 3,000 horses registered worldwide.

Close Call

During World War II, the breed was almost lost. The German Army seized mares and foals from Austria, Italy, and Yugoslavia, and held them at Hostau, in what was Czechoslovakia. General George Patton gave the U.S. Army's protection to the stallions and the Second Cavalry retrieved the mares.

FRIESIAN

NETHERLANDS

The breathtakingly beautiful black Friesian was, in fact, developed as a warhorse in what is now the Netherlands, in northwest Europe. Ancient writings mention that horses like these were used in battle by Friesian troops in Roman Britain, and what would become the modern Friesian breed dates from at least the 1200s.

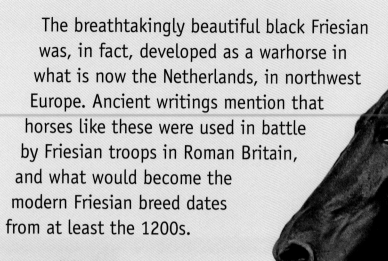

Refined and Proud
During the Crusades, the Friesian was undoubtedly influenced by Arabian and Spanish blood. This shows in its refined head, proud bearing, and high-stepping knee action. However, it has not been influenced by the Thoroughbred and, during the past two centuries, it has been kept pure.

KNOWN FOR:
- Dressage
- Showjumping
- Driving

Elegant and Athletic

The coal-black Friesian was much in demand as a carriage horse and is still seen today pulling hearses at funerals, bearing plumes on its head. But its athletic ability also makes it suitable for equestrian sports, including dressage and Western riding.

In the late 1600s, the breed was taken to America by the Dutch in the settlement called New Amsterdam, now New York.

Heavy Armor

Knights of old wore heavy armor, so their warhorses had to be extremely strong, yet still agile. The Friesian ticked these boxes, and, during the 15th and 16th centuries, its suppleness and athleticism made it popular in riding schools in France and Spain.

77

HANOVERIAN

GERMANY

This breed is undoubtedly one of the horse world's most impressive success stories. The Hanoverian is a "warmblood"—the result of crossing a heavy **draft** horse with a Thoroughbred. It takes its name from its birthplace in the northern German state of Lower Saxony, the former kingdom of Hanover, which has been breeding horses for 300 years.

Going into Battle
The State Stud of Lower Saxony was established at Celle in 1735. The stud farm's early goal was to produce handsome and athletic horses to pull carriages. Later, these fine creatures were required by the cavalry and artillery, so they still needed great strength and agility.

It wasn't until after World War II that the Hanoverian came into its own as a riding and competition horse. Previously used for riding and farm work, it had to have fine looks and a good gait. It had all these qualities, but also proved a supreme competitor.

KNOWN FOR:
- Dressage
- Showjumping
- Driving

Modern Hanoverian horses have medaled in all Olympic disciplines—taking gold in show jumping, dressage, and eventing.

TRAKEHNER

In the early 18th century, King Wilhelm I of Prussia, in northern Germany, wanted a warhorse that was faster, sounder, and more enduring than those of his enemies. He established a stud farm at Trakehnen in East Prussia, where he crossed the small native mares, called *schwaike,* to Thoroughbreds and Arabians.

The Best Results

Various other bloodlines were used to develop the original Trakehner, but King Wilhelm found that he got the best results—handsome, friendly equines that possessed great athletic ability—with the Thoroughbreds and Arabians. He kept the best stock for breeding, and sold the rest as "riding horses."

Elegant Warmblood

Of all the warmblood breeds, the Trakehner has the most Thoroughbred blood, which shows in its handsome appearance. It is more refined than some of the other warmbloods, with an elegant head, long, graceful neck, and deep, sloping shoulder that allows it to move so freely. Renowned for its elastic paces and "floating" trot, the Trakehner is a much-coveted competition horse.

The breed was almost lost during WWII. The East Prussians fled the Soviet Army with wagons and horses, across the frozen bay of the Baltic Sea. Sadly, fewer than 10% of their Trakehners reached safety in West Germany.

OLDENBURG

The Oldenburg or Oldenburger Horse is named from Lower Saxony, Germany, (formerly the Grand Duchy of Oldenburg), its origins dating back to the 17th century.

Origins

The von Oldenburg family bred war horses from Friesian stock with Turkish, Andalusian and Neapolitan blood, later using Spanish and English stallions to produce elegant high-stepping carriage horses. Hanoverian King George I of England (1660–1727) sent Thoroughbreds to improve them. When automation made carriage horses redundant, Thoroughbred blood helped develop a hard-working farm and all-purpose saddle horse.

Oldenburgs are identified by a brand on the left hip: the letter O and a crown plus the last two numbers of the horse's life number.

Recreational Use

Today's Oldenburgs are compact sport horses, 16 to 17.2hh, usually black, brown, or gray, but also bay and chestnut. They are agile showjumpers and valued dressage horses with excellent gaits.

KNOWN FOR:
- Dressage
- Showjumping
- Driving

Naming

Colts are named patrilineally—the first letter of the son's name is the same as the first letter of the sire's name (Adonis out of Aeolus) and fillies matrilineally, (Artemis out of Ariadne), for example.

SELLE FRANÇAIS

It may be one of the youngest warmblood breeds, but the Selle Français has already made its mark as a supreme competition horse. It wasn't until the 20th century that horses were bred in France specifically for sports rather than for war.

The agile Selle Français is a light horse breed. Light horse breeds generally weigh under 1,500 pounds.

KNOWN FOR:
- Dressage
- Showjumping
- Racing

A Local Mix

Various different local breeds have had some influence on the Selle Français, including Vendéen, Charollais, Limousin, and Charentais. After World War II the French concentrated on breeding a horse for riding, and that is how the *cheval de selle Français*, or "French saddle horse," came about.

Model Looks

Thanks to its mix of Thoroughbred and Anglo-Arab blood, the modern Selle Français, like all warmbloods, is extremely handsome. But those good looks are combined with strength, speed, and intelligence.

The Prototype

The breed originated in Normandy, when breeders imported Thoroughbreds and trotters from England to cross with native stock. Two types emerged: a speedy harness horse known as the French Trotter, and the Anglo-Norman. The Anglo-Norman is recognized as the prototype for the Selle Français.

LUSITANO

PORTUGAL

The Lusitano Horse is from Portugal, its name deriving from the ancient Roman name for the region, Lusitania. Sharing its ancestry with Spain's Andalusian, it also shared this name until 1966.

The Lusitano is also known as the Lusitanian, Portuguese, National, Peninsular, or Betico-lusitano.

War Horses

The Greek historian and soldier Xenophon wrote around 370 B.C. of Iberian horsemen and their horses in war. In 711 A.D., Umayyad Muslims invaded, bringing Barb horses which, crossed with natives, became the Iberian war horse. Philip III of Portugal and IV of Spain (1606–1665) halted Portugal's production of cavalry horses, but breeding continued secretly, preserving what became the modern Lusitano.

Color and Character

Lusitanos are any solid color, averaging 15.2hh, with a thick mane and tail. They are brave, high-spirited, and intelligent, with agile movement and springy action.

KNOWN FOR:
- Dressage
- Showjumping
- Riding

Iberian Horses

Portugal's Lusitano and Spain's Andalusian, both known as Iberian horses, have been present on the Iberian peninsula as far back as 25,000 to 20,000 B.C., evidenced by cave paintings.

ARDENNAIS

FRANCE

The Ardennais or Ardennes Horse is one of the oldest draft breeds, probably descended from horses that roamed the Ardennes area of France, Belgium, and Luxembourg over two million years ago.

Bay and roan are the most common colors, also including chestnut, gray, and palomino, but not black. White markings are a small star or blaze only.

Adaptation

Extra weight and size were added to the breed to develop military horses into heavy draft horses, which now average 15–16hh and weigh 1500–2200lbs.

Military Horses

Described by Julius Caesar (100–44 B.C.) as "rustic, hard and tireless", man used the breed's ancestors in early warfare, during the 11th century Crusades, and later as cavalry mounts and artillery horses. Napoleon (1769–1821) added Arabian blood for endurance and used them in his 1812 Russian Campaign to pull artillery and supplies, a role that continued in World War I. After this, mechanization reduced their use.

KNOWN FOR:
- Showjumping
- Driving

Calm Nature

Despite its size and strength, the Ardennais is calm and tolerant, nimble when working on hilly forest ground and long-striding on flat farmland. It is also used for showing and driving.

PALOMINO

Elvis Presley owned a Palomino called Rising Sun.

It is said that the Palomino's coat shines like a new gold coin, and this color in horses is almost as old as the first equines. The Palomino has been revered since ancient times, treasured by royals, and was brought to the Americas by the conquistadors.

The History

In 15th-century Spain, Queen Isabella adored these golden horses. Even today, the color is sometimes called "Isabella." But the breed is older still—when Richard the Lionheart, King of England in the 1100s, retook Jerusalem in 1192, the defeated leader Saladin gave him two horses—one a gray, the other a golden Palomino.

Color

Many believe that Palomino is a coat color, but in the U.S. it is considered a breed, and its bloodlines are carefully protected. Palominos are bred by crossing a chestnut horse with a cream horse. The color varies from a pale gold to a deep, rich copper, with a white mane and tail.

KNOWN FOR:
· Dressage
· Showjumping
· Riding

Royalty Only

The 500 horses owned by Queen Isabella were known as "Golden Dorado." She sent a stallion and five mares to her viceroy in New Spain (now Mexico) so the breed could prosper in the New World. She valued Palominos so highly that she forbade commoners to own one.

BELGIAN

An ancient breed that dates back to Roman times, this heavy draft horse is also known as the Brabant, after the area of Belgium in which it originated.

A Belgian currently holds the record for the tallest living horse. Big Jake, from Winconsin, U.S.A., measured a remarkable 20 hands 2.75 inches tall at the withers.

Strong and Steady

Built for life on the farm, the compact Belgian has exceptional strength. For centuries, draft horses have undertaken the physical work of clearing and plowing fields, pulling heavy wagons, and hauling logs in forests.

Color

The Belgian's traditional color is chestnut, with a mane that is almost exclusively lighter than the color of the horse.

Different Drafts

The Brabant draft horse is the foundation horse for the American Belgian. Until about 1940, the Brabant and the American Belgian were in effect the same horse. After World War II, the European Brabant was bred to be thicker-bodied, with heavy **feathering** on the legs. After the war, a taller, lighter-bodied horse was founded in the United States.

HAFLINGER

AUSTRIA

A tiny village in the Southern Tyrolean Mountains of what is now Austria and northern Italy gave its name to this enchanting breed. Many of the farms and villages in the area were reachable only by narrow paths and steep mountain trails, which called for an agile and sure-footed horse.

KNOWN FOR:
- Dressage
- Showjumping
- Racing

Perfect for Pack

There is no carthorse blood in the Haflinger. Sturdy carthorses would not have been much use in the Tyrol. The compact Haflinger was ideally suited to working on the high mountain farms, and the steep fields and forests. They were excellent pack animals, used to transport food between farms and villages, and are still used today for pack or lumber work.

From the Tyrol mountains, the Haflinger has spread to 60 countries, with 250,000 horses registered.

Charming Horse

In addition to its glorious color, the Haflinger is a charming creature, with an endearing, people-loving nature. It is willing to work, which makes it very child-friendly, and can turn its hoof to almost any equestrian discipline.

The First Stallion

The Haflinger—named after the village of Hafling—is Middle Eastern in origin. The foundation stallion was 249 Folie, who was foaled in 1874. Folie was by an Arabian stallion out of a native Tyrolean mare. All modern Haflingers can be traced back to Folie through seven different stallion lines.

PERCHERON

FRANCE

Of all the heavy horse breeds, the Percheron must be the most elegant, a trait that comes from its Arabian heritage. It was originally bred at Le Perche, in Normandy, France, and was probably introduced to England by William the Conqueror in 1066. But its origins are thought to date back to the 8th century.

KNOWN FOR:
- Dressage
- Showjumping
- Racing

The Arab Influence
The high proportion of Arabian blood in this heavy horse breed is evident in its fine head and in its color—it is always gray or black. It has the wide forehead, wide nostrils, and long neck seen in the Arab. Its legs have less hair than other draft breeds, with a powerful forearm and muscular thighs. Its lively action and high-set tail also tell of its exotic breeding.

American Studbook

The first Percherons were imported to the U.S. in 1839 by Edward Harris of Moorestown, New Jersey. He twice tried to bring in eight horses, but only two survived the journey— a mare called Joan and a stallion named Diligence. The stallion lived up to his name, siring more than 400 offspring.

From War Horse to Farm Horse

The early horses carried knights wearing heavy armor into battle. But a lighter horse was later required for working the land. The founding stallion was named Jean Le Blanc, the offspring of a local draft mare and an Arabian sire called Gallipoly, foaled in 1823. The Arabian blood gave the breed its high-stepping action and refined good looks.

The first American Percheron studbook was opened in 1876.

FJORD

NORWAY

Around 4,000 years ago, the horses that were found in Norway, Scandinavia, were first domesticated by humans. Remains found at Viking burial sites indicate that the Fjord has been selectively bred for 2,000 years. Today, this strong and resilient little horse is one of Norway's national symbols.

KNOWN FOR:
- Dressage
- Showjumping
- Riding

Primitive Markings
The attractive Fjord is nearly always dun in color, often showing the "wild" markings of striped legs, black points, and a black dorsal stripe down its back.

High Regard

"The eyes should be like the mountain lakes on a midsummer evening, big and bright. A bold bearing of the neck, like a lad from the mountains on his way to his beloved. The temperament as lively as a waterfall in spring, and still good-natured," reads a famous, anonymous Norwegian description of the Fjord breed.

Unique to the Fjord is its striking mane. The mane is cut short into a crescent shape. The white outer hair is trimmed just shorter than the dark inner hair to display the dramatic dark stripe.

It is likely that the Fjord is related to the Asiatic Wild Horse.

ICELANDIC

ICELAND

Though the size of a pony, the Icelandic is a horse; in fact, there is no word for "pony" in the Icelandic language. Small, strong, and tough, it is the only horse breed in Iceland, earning the label "most useful servant."

A "Pure" Breed

No horses can be imported into Iceland, and exported Icelandic horses are not allowed back, a policy that keeps the breed "pure" and limits introduced diseases.

Myth

The Icelandic is descended from horses taken to Iceland by settlers on Norse ships over 1000 years ago. Horses are venerated in Norse mythology and include Sleipnir, the 8-footed horse of the chief god, Odin. Horses used in battle were so revered that they were often buried with their fallen riders.

In pacing races, Icelandics doing the "flying pace" reach speeds of up to 30 mph, racing on land in summer and on ice in winter.

WELSH

WALES, U.K.

Arabian influence is clear to see in the pretty head of the Welsh Mountain pony. Its wide forehead, large eyes, and dished profile give it an Arab-type appearance. This probably dates back to Roman times, when the invading armies brought horses that had been captured during their African campaigns. They left them behind when they withdrew in 410 A.D.

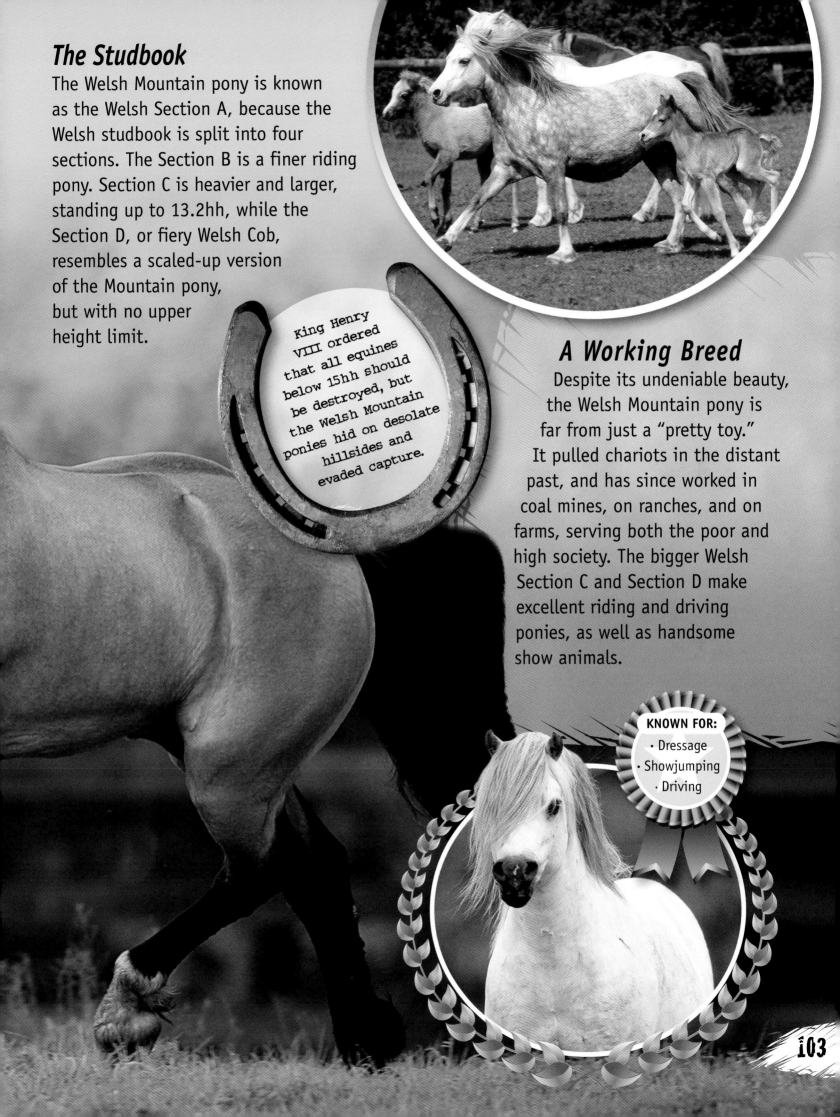

The Studbook

The Welsh Mountain pony is known as the Welsh Section A, because the Welsh studbook is split into four sections. The Section B is a finer riding pony. Section C is heavier and larger, standing up to 13.2hh, while the Section D, or fiery Welsh Cob, resembles a scaled-up version of the Mountain pony, but with no upper height limit.

King Henry VIII ordered that all equines below 15hh should be destroyed, but the Welsh Mountain ponies hid on desolate hillsides and evaded capture.

A Working Breed

Despite its undeniable beauty, the Welsh Mountain pony is far from just a "pretty toy." It pulled chariots in the distant past, and has since worked in coal mines, on ranches, and on farms, serving both the poor and high society. The bigger Welsh Section C and Section D make excellent riding and driving ponies, as well as handsome show animals.

KNOWN FOR:
- Dressage
- Showjumping
- Driving

HIGHLAND

SCOTLAND, U.K.

The Highland Pony, native to Scotland, is one of the largest mountain and moorland breeds. It developed in the harsh, inhospitable Highlands, over centuries, becoming perfectly suited to its location.

Development

Hardy and sure-footed on rocky ground, this ancient breed developed on the mainland and Western Isles, which include Harris and Lewis, Barra, and North Uist. The summer coat is replaced by strong hairs over a soft, dense undercoat in winter.

KNOWN FOR:
- Riding
- Showjumping
- Endurance riding

Colors

Highland ponies are gray, chestnut, bay, and dun, the latter with "primitive markings": a dorsal stripe down the center back, some with zebra-stripes on the inside forelegs. The mane and tail are long and flowing, the legs feathered, and the white markings limited to a small star.

Strangely, Highland Ponies rarely need shoeing, or stable rugs.

Helpful Horse

In extreme conditions crofters—people that rented small pieces of land on an estate—relied on the Highland Pony for transport, hauling timber, plowing, and carrying game—they hauled and carried huge weights for their 13–14.2hh height. Quiet and willing, they were cheap to keep, and largely disease-free.

SHETLAND

SCOTLAND, U.K.

Tiny ponies have lived on the Shetlands—the northernmost islands of the United Kingdom—for over 2,000 years. Their origins probably lie in the ancient tundra ponies that walked across the ice fields and land masses during the last Ice Age, thousands of years ago.

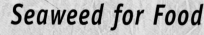

Seaweed for Food

Few horses were imported to the isolated Shetland Isles, so the pony remained pure for centuries. No place in Shetland is farther than four miles from the sea, and it is local legend that, during the worst winters, ponies would forage for seaweed along the shoreline.

Oriental Influence

The Celtic people, who came to Great Britain over the period from about 500 B.C. to 100 B.C., brought with them other equines, probably with Eastern blood. They bred these to the native animals and the result was a small, strong, and hardy pony that worked alongside its island owners.

Highly Prized

The ponies worked the land, carried peat and seaweed, and survived on meager rations. Fishermen would even use hairs from their tails as fishing line. For all these things, the Shetland was highly prized.

One of the earliest laws recorded in Shetland cautioned would-be thieves not to "cut any other man's horse-tail or mane under the pain [of a fine] of ten pounds"— a huge sum of money in those days.

HACKNEY

ENGLAND, U.K.

The Hackney is a general-purpose, reliable breed, with good stamina. Intelligent and attractive, it is noted for its high-stepping trot. Hackneys are allowed at both horse and pony heights, one of the few breeds to recognize both.

This breed has a broad chest and long, strong shoulders with powerful hind quarters, the tail set and carried high.

Royal Connections

The Hackney was developed in Great Britain from the 14th century, to meet the desire for powerful but attractive horses with a good trotting action. From 1542 King Henry VII required wealthy subjects to keep trotting horses for breeding, and Henry VIII and Elizabeth I continued to favor the breed. The word Hackney derives from the French "haquenee," a comfortable riding style.

Hackneys have a well-shaped head and alert eyes and ears.

High Steppers

In the Regency period (1811–1820), smart, elegant Hackneys were highly prized as both riding and carriage horses for their brisk, springy walk and high-stepping trot, with sharply bent knees. Hackneys are reported as trotting 16–20 miles in an hour, and covering 50–60 miles in a day.

KNOWN FOR:
- Dressage
- Showjumping
- Driving

CLEVELAND BAY

ENGLAND, U.K.

The Cleveland Bay is England's oldest breed of horse. Its history is said to predate written records. Developing from pack horses crossed with other blood, it became a very versatile breed, though it is now rare.

War Service

Cleveland Bays proved their worth as the mounts of troopers and as artillery horses on the battlefields of World War I, where many died.

Royal Support

In 1961 Queen Elizabeth II bought the stallion Mulgrave Supreme to prevent his export, and made him available for breeding to support the breed. Cleveland Bays still pull carriages in Royal processions, and were used by the Duke of Edinburgh for carriage driving.

KNOWN FOR:
- Dressage
- Showjumping
- Driving

Origins

The name derives from the breed's origins in the Cleveland area of Yorkshire, northern England, and its color, bay. Strong, reliable horses were needed by riders, carters, and farmers, and to pull coaches, and the Cleveland Bay met this need for endurance and stamina combined with an easy temperament.

Buffalo Bill Cody was a big Cleveland Bay fan, driving four in his Wild West Show.

CONNEMARA

Ireland's west coast is wild, rocky, and wave-lashed by the Atlantic Ocean. Connemara ponies have lived there for centuries, scraping an existence from desolate moors, bogs, and barren coastline. This sure-footed, hardy pony is now considered Ireland's only native breed.

The modern Connemara is a strong riding pony, with good jumping ability.

KNOWN FOR:
- Dressage
- Showjumping
- Driving

In Demand

Today the Connemara pony is much in demand. Good-looking and gentle, it retains the athleticism from its mountain life. A wonderful child's pony, it is also popular in the show ring.

The Legend

Celtic warriors brought their dun-colored ponies to the island around 2,500 years ago. Some broke free, and a wild pony population soon roamed the ancient mountains. Legend says that when the Spanish Armada sank off the Connemara coast in the 16th century, some Spanish horses swam to shore and mated with the native stock.

A Hard Life

If life was tough for Connemara's ponies, it was doubly so for the region's struggling farmers. For some, the only option to get a decent pony was to capture and tame one from the mountain—preferably a mare who could provide a foal to sell.

SUFFOLK

ENGLAND, U.K.

Britain's oldest heavy horse breed is the Suffolk. All modern
Suffolks can be traced back to one stallion, called Crisp's Horse of
Ufford. Foaled in 1768, he is considered the breed's foundation sire,
but he was not actually the first Suffolk. These animals were first bred
as huge, heavy war horses, but the breed was shaped by the land it
worked on in Norfolk and Suffolk in the east of England.

Short and Stocky
The Suffolk is smaller than other draft breeds and,
unlike the Shire, has no "feather"—long, silky hair—
on its lower legs. This would not be helpful in the sticky clay of
its home counties. The Suffolk was initially unaffected by the
coming of motorized tractors, because few of the early machines
could cope with the local clay soil.

Working the Land

The Suffolk's birthplace is bordered by the North Sea, and on the west by the fens—low-lying, flat marshland that was drained for farming. The farmers here needed a strong, docile, and long-living horse to plow the heavy clay soil. The fenland farmers made their living from their crops, not the horses they bred, so the Suffolk remained fairly pure.

The Suffolk is always chestnut—ranging from bright golden to dark liver.

Suffolk Punch

The handsome Suffolk has a square, solid appearance, braced on short, sturdy legs. This "leg-at-each-corner" stance gave the breed its nickname of "Suffolk Punch." It has a fairly small, intelligent head, arching neck, and a short, strong back.

SHIRE

ENGLAND, U.K.

England's most famous heavy draft breed takes its name from the Saxon word *schyran*, meaning "to shear, or divide." Its English form, shire, appears on the end of many British county names. The draft horse was descended from heavy war horses and was first called a Shire by Henry VIII in the early 16th century.

The Shire had previously been known as the "Great Horse," the "Cart-Horse," the "English Black," and the "Lincolnshire Giant."

Industrial Revolution

As roads improved during the 18th century, the Shire became much in demand for draft work, as well as pulling plows on farms, where it had replaced oxen. During the Industrial Revolution, a nationwide network of canals was built, so horses were needed to walk along the banks, pulling the barges.

A Bleak Outlook

The Industrial Revolution almost proved to be the Shire's downfall, however. As trains replaced barges, and tractors replaced plows, the mighty horses fell out of favor. Numbers dropped from more than a million to just a few thousand in the 1960s.

Shire Success Story

In England, a small group of dedicated breeders saved valuable bloodlines and kept the breed going. Today, the Shire Horse Society is in good shape, holding an annual show. Shire enthusiasts visit from the world over to celebrate the mighty horse.

CLYDESDALE

SCOTLAND, U.K.

Once one of the smallest draft horses, Scotland's Clydesdale (sometimes called Clyde in the U.S.) has been developed into one of the most impressive, powerful, and recognizable breeds, often seen at shows and in parades.

Handsome
Clydesdales have a wide muzzle, large nostrils, bright eyes, and large ears. The lower legs have extensive feathering, and gaits are active, with hooves clearly lifted, giving an overall impression of great power.

Bred for Power

The name "Clydesdale" was first recorded in 1826. Developed from Flemish stallions imported into Scotland crossed with local mares, the breed's huge power was developed for farm work, and hauling coal, logs, and heavy goods. Large numbers were exported—over 20,000 between 1884 and 1945, many to New Zealand and Australia, earning the label "The breed that built Australia."

KNOWN FOR:
- Dressage
- Showjumping
- Driving

Spectacle

Clydesdales are used by the British Household Cavalry as drum horses on state and ceremonial occasions. They must be a minimum of 17hh, carrying a Musical Ride Officer and two silver drums each weighing 123lb.

This large breed eats twice as much as other horses—between 25 and 50lb of hay a day, plus about 5lb of concentrated feed.

ORLOV TROTTER

After the Russian Emperor Peter III was assassinated in 1762, his wife took the throne as Catherine the Great. As thanks for his role in this coup, Count Alexei Orlov was given land in the steppe region of central Russia. It was here that Count Orlov founded the Khrenovsky Stud, where the Orlov breed was later developed. The farm is still in operation today.

The Beautiful Breed

The Orlov Trotter was bred to be a harness horse of great speed and beauty. The Count's wealth, popularity, and political connections enabled him to acquire the very best horses from Arabia, Persia, and Europe. Among these was the Arabian stallion Smetanka, who was silver-gray and long-backed.

Experiments

After some experiments, the Count bred Smetanka to a dun-colored Danish mare, producing a gray stallion called Polkan I in 1778. When Smetanka died, the Count bred his son, Polkan, to Friesian mares, including an unusual gray. The resulting son, a gray called Bars I, foaled in 1784, is regarded as the foundation sire for the breed.

An autopsy after the stallion Smetanka's death revealed that he had an extra rib.

Sporting Prowess

Traditionally, the Orlov was a handsome carriage horse, but it was also in demand for the troika, a sled-type vehicle pulled by three horses. The center horse trots, while the two outside horses gallop. In modern times, the Orlov has shown its skill in sporting events, including the Olympic Games.

KNOWN FOR:
- Dressage
- Showjumping
- Driving

121

MARWARI

INDIA

This beautiful horse comes from a time of castles and heroes, intrigue and passion, dark deeds and mythology. The elegant Marwari captures the essence of a "period when horses had wings." This may not be true, but the Marwari was held in high regard in its native India, where it had been known since at least the 12th century.

Homing Instinct

As well as its speed and beauty, the Marwari is renowned for its homing instinct. It saved the lives of countless riders, when they became lost in the desert. Its tiny ears had excellent hearing, too—it could pick up sounds of danger before any human.

Banished to the Desert

The Rathores were the first to breed the Marwari, and were proud of their great cavalry of more than 50,000 horses. The Marwari was noted for its loyalty and bravery in battle, a breed that would lay down its life for its master.

KNOWN FOR:
- Riding
- Showjumping
- Endurance riding

The modern Marwari makes a popular safari horse, because of its loyalty, gentleness, and smooth, comfortable gait.

The Marwari Today

As the role of the horse in battle declined, so did the Marwaris' numbers. Under British rule, the breed was almost lost. However, in 1998, the Maharaja Gaj Singh II founded the All India Marwari Horse Society to preserve India's national horse.

CASPIAN

IRAN

In 1965, an American named Louise Firouz discovered herds of small horses living in northern Iran. These little creatures were horses, not ponies, yet they stood less than 12hh, and were thought to have been extinct for 1,000 years. Firouz named them Caspian horses.

Caspians may be ancestors to the ancient Arabian.

Horses of Kings

Ancient artifacts show that the ancient kings of this region used small, elegant horses. They pulled the chariots of King Darius the Great, who ruled from 522 to 486 B.C. A frieze at his palace near modern Tehran features small horses that reach only to their leaders' waists. Once known as *Lydean* horses, they were undoubtedly the first Caspians.

Gift Horses

Firouz established a herd of Caspians at her riding school just outside Tehran. Of these, seven mares and six stallions became the foundation stock for a breeding center. In 1971, a mare and a stallion were presented to Prince Philip, the husband of the British queen, Elizabeth II. A respected horseman, he recommended that more Caspians be exported to the U.K., Australia, and New Zealand, and the ancient breed was saved.

KNOWN FOR:
- Dressage
- Showjumping
- Racing

A Living Link

More recently, small, delicate equines were seen along the southern shores of the Caspian Sea, as well as in the mountains and villages around it. They were known locally as *Mouleki* or *Pouseki* ponies and were used for pack or pulling carts.

AUSTRALIAN STOCK HORSE

AUSTRALIA

Horses are not native to Australia, and when the country was settled by Europeans in the 18th century, they introduced the first horses, to be developed to meet the country's specific needs.

"The Breed for Every Need"

Tough conditions required tough horses. Under saddle and in harness, settlers and stockmen needed hardy, agile horses of sound temperament to clear timber, pull plows, and herd cattle and sheep on huge "stations," often traveling long distances day after day. What became the Australian Stock Horse met these needs. They could race, too!

Origins

When British ships arrived to settle Australia in the 1780s, among the cargo were nine horses, a mix of breeds including Thoroughbred, Arabian, and Welsh Mountain Pony. They had to survive the long, arduous sea journey, and also adapt to work in an unfamiliar landscape and climate. Only the strongest were allowed to breed, with more Thoroughbreds and American Quarter Horses being introduced to improve the stock.

During the 2000 Sydney Olympics opening ceremony, over 100 Australian Stock Horses were paraded, performing maneuvers to music.

A NEW LIFE BEGINS

All baby animals are adorable, but there's something about a newborn foal's wide-eyed gawkiness that captures the heart—whether it represents the next generation of a racing dynasty, or that of a much-loved family pony.

A young Exmoor Pony foal.

A Baby at Risk

A newborn foal is especially vulnerable, and so is its mother. Mares tend to give birth at night, or very early in the morning—the quietest time of day. In the wild, a mare will give birth at night because she can hide her foal in the darkness until it is able to run away from predators. Even today, a mare may delay foaling until nighttime, when she feels most safe.

The gestation period lasts for about eleven months, or about 340 days (normal average range 320–370 days).

A pair of beautiful Appaloosa foals.

Finding their Feet

When wild horses roamed freely in forests and grasslands, they were prey animals, not predators. A horse has two basic defense mechanisms—fight or flight—and it mostly relies on the latter. Over thousands of years, horses have evolved into tall animals that use their long legs to outrun hunters.

129

Learning to Stand

A foal is born weak and unsteady, but after about 30 minutes it will try to stand. In the wild, this is vital, since it must be able to flee with its mother if danger threatens. It may make several attempts to stand, wobbling on its spindly legs before toppling to the ground. An hour after birth, the foal is steady on its feet.

Morgan foals at play.

Welsh Ponies: a mare and foal.

A foal will taste grass when they are about a week old. Foals nurse for about 4–6 months, but they can be weaned from their mother's milk after a year.

Survival Instincts

Once it is able to stand for more than a few seconds, the foal will take its first, shaky steps. Its first action is to seek its mother's udder to suckle, taking in the nutrients needed for survival. About two hours after it is born, the foal will be able to trot and gallop.

A Shetland foal learns to stand.

Growing Up

For the first month or so the foal will stay close to its mother, but as it gets braver and more confident, it will leave her side to play. If there are other mares and foals, it will interact with them. The foals will engage in mock battles, rearing, striking out with their feet, and running away.

A Morgan foal, bucking and kicking.

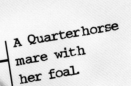

A Quarterhorse mare with her foal.

Learning to Survive

Although the foal's antics may look carefree, it is learning all the time. Bucking, kicking, and galloping strengthens its bones and muscles. As it spins and twists, it learns how to use its body to stay balanced. All this prepares the foal for its future— but hopefully not to flee the danger that stalked its ancestors.

FEEDING

Horses are herbivores that eat plants, especially grass. Living naturally, they graze for up to 20 hours a day. Horses are "Trickle feeders"—they need to top up with food regularly as they have small stomachs in relation to their size.

Hay may not look like much, but it is excellent food, providing calcium, vitamins, protein, and fiber.

At Grass

In fine weather when grazing is plentiful, horses at grass may not need the supplementary feeding required in harsh, cold weather, or when they are working hard.

Water

All horses need a constant supply of clean, fresh water. They drink between five to ten gallons per day.

Bulk and Concentrate

Domesticated horses need bulk food or roughage in the form of hay (dried grass) to keep them feeling satisfied, and concentrates like barley and oats for energy. Apples and carrots help digestion. Ready-mixed as cubes or nuts, compound feeds provide a scientifically balanced diet.

GROOMING

Grooming is essential for all horses, helping to keep them healthy by removing dust, hair, and other debris, and maintaining the skin and coat in good condition.

Full Groom

Stabled horses need a full groom every day. This involves picking stones from the feet with a hoof pick and brushing the neck, head, body, mane and tail with dandy and body brushes, and a curry comb. Eyes, nose, and lips are sponged with warm water, and the coat is polished with a stable rubber. Finally, hooves are painted with hoof oil.

At Grass

Wild horses and those at grass groom themselves, rolling, shaking, or rubbing against trees or fences. They also use their lips and teeth to groom each other. They need grease in the coat to keep them warm and dry, and do not need much grooming. A dandy brush, foot pick, and sponge for the face are all that's required.

Benefits

Brushing gets rid of grease and dirt from skin pores, so horses sweat freely. It helps blood under the skin flow well, and keeps the coat smooth and glossy.

A grooming kit includes dandy; body and water brushes; mane and curry combs; hoof pick and oil; sweat scraper; sponges, and stable rubber.

TACK AND EQUIPMENT

Tack are the pieces of equipment used with domesticated horses. When man first began to ride horses, he used only a very simple bridle—saddles and stirrups appeared much later.

A saddle pad is a pad made of natural material fitted under the saddle to keep horses comfortable and absorb sweat.

Tack

Equipping a horse is called tacking up, and a place where equipment is stored is a tack room. Tack should fit well, and includes a saddle, and a seat for the rider fastened to the horse's back by a strap called a cinch in Western style (a girth in English-style) riding. Stirrups hang down either side to support the rider's feet.

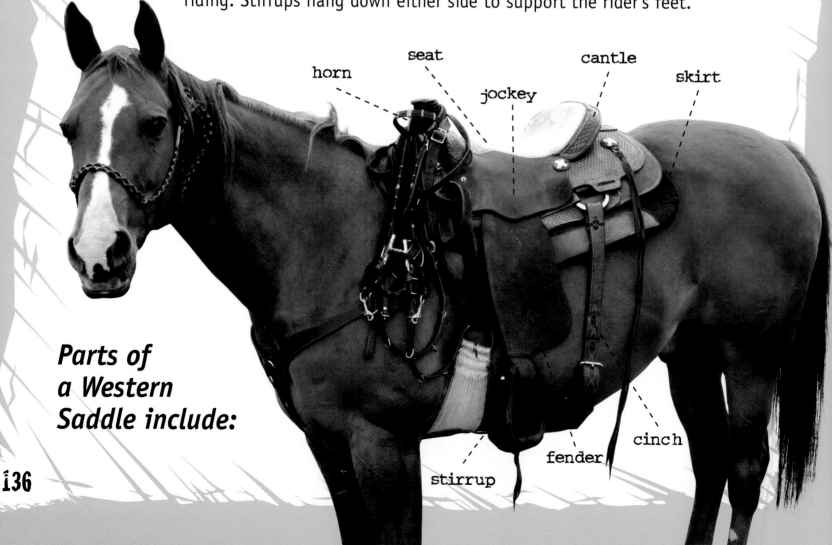

horn
seat
cantle
jockey
skirt
cinch
fender
stirrup

Parts of a Western Saddle include:

Extras

Rugs can be worn to keep off flies or in cold or wet weather. Bandages protect and support lower legs, and boots protect legs from injury.

Cleanliness

Tack must be cleaned regularly—leather washed, dried, and rubbed with saddle soap; metal parts washed and polished, except for the bit, which is washed only.

Headgear

Headgear comprises a bridle, an arrangement of straps used to control the horse's head, and reins—leather straps or rope—attached to a bit in the horse's mouth. The rider uses the reins to communicate directional commands—to steer or stop.

Parts of a Bridle include:

headpiece

throatlash

browband

cheekpiece

noseband

bit

rein

GLOSSARY

action
The way a horse or pony moves—"high action" or "low action," depending where the legs are in relation to the ground.

Akhal-Teke
Ancient breed of horse originating in Turkmenistan.

Andalusian
A pure Spanish horse, which influenced breeding worldwide.

Appaloosa
An American breed, known for its colorful spotted coat.

Arabian
Ancient breed, from the Middle East. It has a strong influence on many other breeds, including the Thoroughbred.

Ardennais
An ancient breed of draft horse from France and Belgium.

Australian Stock Horse
A hardy Australian horse, bred for endurance.

Belgian
A heavy draft horse from the Brabant region, in Belgium.

blanket
A solid white area usually over the hip area with a contrasting base coat.

brindle
A tiger-striped coat pattern with irregular streaks of color.

Brumby
A free-roaming Australian horse.

Camargue
An ancient breed of horse from France's Camargue region.

Caspian
A small horse breed, native to Northern Iran.

chestnuts
Rough patches on the inner leg, compared to human fingerprints.

Chincoteague Pony
A breed of wild pony living on Assateague Island, U.S.

Cleveland Bay
A bay horse that originated in England, U.K.

coldblood
Large, strong breeds of horse from northern Europe.

colt
An uncastrated male horse up to four years of age. Male foals are called "colt foals."

competition horse
A horse bred for competitions, such as eventing, dressage, or showjumping.

conformation
A horse or pony's overall shape and proportions.

Connemara Pony
A hardy pony breed, originating in Ireland.

coronet
A narrow band or marking, just above the hoof.

draft horse
A heavy horse, bred for work or farm labor.

dressage
The advanced training of a horse, performed in competitions.

driving
An equestrian sport with different types of competition.

dun
A coat color—yellow or sandy-colored body with black points.

Equidae
Species that belong to the horse family.

eventing
A competition including dressage, cross-country, and showjumping.

Exmoor Pony
A hardy pony, native to England, U.K. Some are semi-feral.

Falabella
A miniature horse from Argentina.

feather
The long hair that grows on the lower part of a heavy horse's legs. Also present on some ponies.

fetlock
The joint on a lower part of a horse's leg, just above the foot.

feral
A free-roaming horse with domesticated ancestors.

filly
Female horse under four years old. A female foal is called a "filly foal."

Fjord
A small, strong mountain horse from Norway.

foal
A colt, filly or gelding up to one year of age.

Friesian
A graceful horse from the Netherlands.

gait
The paces at which horses move, usually the walk, trot, canter, and gallop.

gaited
Horse breeds developed for natural gaited (smooth-to-ride) abilities.

Haflinger
A sturdy horse breed, from the South Tyrol, Austria.

hands
Unit of measure used to describe a horse. One hand (1 hh) equals 4 inches.

Hanoverian
A German warmblood, bred for competition.

heavy horse
A large draft horse. The Shire and the Belgian Draft are among them.

Highland
A hardy mountain pony, native to Scotland, U.K.

hotbloods
A term that describes horses of Arabian or Thoroughbred blood.

Icelandic
A sturdy, pony-sized horse, developed in Iceland.

Jennet
A now-extinct breed
of Spanish horse.

Lippizaner
Elegant European horse,
associated with the Spanish
Riding School in Austria.

Lusitano
A Portuguese breed, related
to the Andalusian.

Mangalarga Marchador
A breed adapted as the
national horse of Brazil.

mare
A female horse over
the age of three.

Marwari
A rare breed from the
Marwar region of India.

Missouri Foxtrotter
Breed of gaited horse
developed in Missouri's
mountain region.

Morgan Horse
An American breed,
developed in the late
18th century.

Mustang
A wild horse from
America's West.

New Forest Pony
One of Great Britain's
native breeds, originating
in the New Forest.

Oldenburg
A warmblood breed
from Saxony, Germany.

Orlov Trotter
A breed of horse from
Russia. Used for draft work,
competition and pleasure.

Paint
An American stock horse
crossed with a pinto.

Palomino
Coat color in which the
body can be shades of
gold, with a silver or
white mane and tail.

Paso Fino
A breed, originally from
Spain, known for its
comfortable gait.

passport
Documentation that
identifies a horse by
its height and breed.

pastern
The part of the leg
between the fetlock,
and the top of the hoof.

Percheron
A popular draft horse breed,
from northern France.

Peruvian Paso
A breed originating from
Spanish stock. Peru's
national horse.

piebald
A body color of white
with black patches.

Pinto
A coat color of white with
patches of another color.

points
The physical features
of a horse.

Pony of the Americas
An American pony breed,
developed in Iowa.

Quarter Horse
A breed of horse,
originating in the U.S.
Used for ranch work,
racing, and competition.

racehorse
A horse bred for racing,
often warmbloods and
Thoroughbreds.

roan
Coat color in which white
hairs are mixed with the
base coat color.

Rocky Mountain Horse
A hardy breed developed in Kentucky, U.S.

Saddlebred
An impressive breed from the U.S. Known for its spectacular gaits.

sclera
The white of the eye.

Selle Français
A French horse, bred for competition.

Shetland Pony
A small pony breed, native to the Shetland Isles, north of Scotland, U.K.

Shire Horse
A breed of draft horse, originating in England. Used as a war horse, and later for farm labor.

showjumping
A jumping competition at a horse show.

skewbald
A coat with irregular patches of white and another color.

stallion
An uncastrated male horse.

studbook
A book kept by a breed society or registry in which eligible horses are recorded.

Suffolk
An English draft horse, always chestnut in color.

tack
The equipment used for riding—saddle, bridle, etc. Short for "tackle."

temperament
A horse or pony's nature, ranging from calm and docile to unpredictable.

Thoroughbred
A breed developed in England. Used as a racehorse and to refine other breeds.

Trakehner
A breed of warmblood horse, used for a variety of competition events.

warmbloods
A group of middle-weight horse types and breeds, originating in Europe.

Welsh Pony
An ancient mountain pony, from Wales, U.K.

withers
The ridge at the base of the horse's neck, from which the horse's height is measured.

whorl
A mark or patch of hair growing on a horse's head.

INDEX

PICTURE CREDITS

Images, unless specified, are courtesy of Bob Langrish.

In January 2011, Bob Langrish was awarded an M.B.E. (Member of the Order of the British Empire) by the Queen, for Equestrian Photography and Services to Art, having completely illustrated around 150 books on horses. This award has only ever been given to a handful of photographers ever and no one specializing in equine photography.

Bob Langrish works for equine magazines in more than 20 countries and travels extensively all over the world to obtain 400,000 plus images in his library of pictures.

Additional images:
Key: t = top, c = center, b = bottom, l = left, r = right, m = main, bg = background, fc = front cover

Getty images
54b DEA/B. Langrish; 54–55 DEA/B. Langrish; 55r DEA/B. Langrish; 83r Tim Graham; 89b DEA/B. Langrish; 104–105; 108–109 DEA/B. Langrish.

Shutterstock
horseshoe/Vaclav Volrab, rosettes/VectorPic, laurel wreath/Igor Shikov.
4bg withGod; 8m mariait; 9tl Nina B; 9tc Rita Kochmarjova; 10m Eric Isselee; 10-11bg, 138–141bg Iakov Kalinin. 12br Stephanie; Coffman; 13c elj92-d38tgll; 14tr Savo Ilic, 14br Sara Julin Ingelmark; 15br Bastiaan Schuit; 16cr Karel Gallas; 16bl Bildagentur Zoonar GmbH; 17tr olgaru79; 18bg Bear designer; 18br olgaru79; 19t horsemen; 19c olgaru79; 19b olgaru79; 59tr Margo Harrison; 74c Best dog photo; 79c Abramova Kseniya; 81t Julia Remezova; 82m Abramova Kseniya; 82t Rita Kochmarjova; 83t olgaru79; 86m Olga_i; 86b Ricardo Furtado; 87t Ricardo Furtado; 87b K. Kolygo; 88m Carole Castelli; 89t Carole Castelli; 92m Sari ONeal; 93t Reinhard Tiburzy; 93b Sari ONeal; 94c horsemen; 96c Perry Correll; 100m Nina B;
100t Karel Cerny; 101t Jeannette Katzir Photog; 104m oceanwhisper;
104c Vera Zinkova; 105b life_in_a_pixel; 109b i4lcocl2;
110m Nicole Ciscato; 110c Nicole Ciscato; 118m photo-equine;
119t Horse Crazy; 119c Nicole Ciscato; 121b horsemen;
126m Regien Paassen; 127t John Carnemolla; 127b John Carnemolla;
130m,144b mariait; 132m Svietlieisha Olena; 133t rancho;
133b Duncan Andison; 134c Horse Crazy; 134t michaelheim;
134b Vicki L. Miller; 135t Budimir Jevtic; 136 Flaxphotos;
137tl Sheikoevgeniya; 137tr Christopher Meder; 137b bagicat